**Ela Area** ✎ **S0-AWH-830**
275 Mohawk Trail, Lake Zurich, IL 60047
(847) 438-3433
www.eapl.org

31241008954748

JUN – – 2017

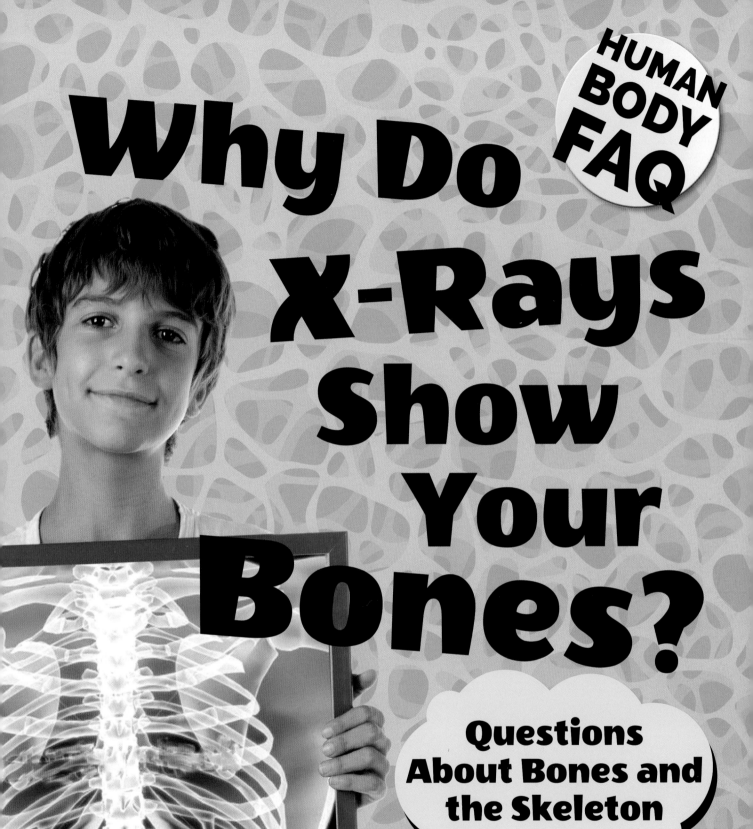

HUMAN BODY FAQ

# Why Do X-Rays Show Your Bones?

**Questions About Bones and the Skeleton**

by **Thomas Canavan**

**PowerKiDS** press.

Published in 2017 by **The Rosen Publishing Group, Inc.**
29 East 21st Street, New York, NY 10010

Cataloging-in-Publication Data

Names: Canavan, Thomas.
Title: Why do x-rays show your bones? / Thomas Canavan.
Description: New York : PowerKids Press, 2017. | Series: Human body FAQ | Includes index.
Identifiers: ISBN 9781499431735 (pbk.) | ISBN 9781499432268 (library bound) |
 ISBN 9781499431742 (6 pack)
Subjects: LCSH: Bones--Juvenile literature. | Skeleton--Juvenile literature.
Classification: LCC QM101.C317 2017 | DDC 573.7'6--dc23

Copyright © 2017 Arcturus Holdings Limited

Author: Thomas Canavan
Designers: Supriya Sahai and Emma Randall
Editors: Joe Harris and Anna Brett

Picture credits: Cover illustration: Shutterstock. Interior illustrations: Shutterstock

All rights reserved. No part of this book may be reproduced in any form without
permission in writing from the publisher, except by a reviewer.

Manufactured in the United States of America
CPSIA Compliance Information: Batch #BW17PK: For Further Information contact Rosen Publishing, New York, New York at 1-800-237-9932.

# Contents

# How is your body like a building?

Every building needs protection on the outside, and strong supports running through it to keep it from toppling over. Your body is just the same. Without the support provided by your bones, you'd flop over like a rag doll. The framework of bones is called the skeleton.

## Are all your bones joined together?
Most of the bones in your skeleton are linked but your hyoid bone, in your throat, is not connected to any other bones.

# What does your skeleton protect?

Your body contains many delicate organs such as the heart, lungs, and brain. It hurts even if your tough outer layers get bumped. Things would be far worse if your skeleton didn't protect your sensitive internal organs.

## How have humans changed?

Modern humans have more delicate bones and rounder heads than our ancestors who lived 4 million years ago.

# How do our bones tell a story?

Most parts of a body decompose (break down) after a person dies. Bones take much longer to decompose, and can even become fossils, so they can tell us about our ancestors many thousands or even millions of years ago. Scientists can tell how humans have changed and what type of injuries and illnesses ancient humans faced.

# How many bones are there in your body?

A human adult skeleton contains 206 bones. There are several types of bones. Your fingers, toes, arms, and legs contain long bones. Your wrists and feet have short bones for support and stability. Flat bones, including your hips, ribs, and shoulder blades, are strong for protecting vital organs.

## What is your spine made of?

A human spine has 33 disc-shaped backbones, called vertebrae, linked in a long line. They form a tunnel through the middle to protect your spinal cord. Most mammals have seven of these bones in their neck section, whether they are as tiny as a mouse or as tall as a giraffe!

## What is the smallest bone in the body?

The smallest bone is the 0.11-inch (2.8 mm) stirrup bone, which is found in the ear.

# Can we change our bones?

Eating the right foods helps to make your bones strong and hard. Exercise also strengthens bones. Over time, the bones of athletes become tougher and thicker. A right-handed tennis player often has longer bones in their right arm than left arm.

## How many bones do we have in our head?

Your brain is protected by eight flat, bony plates, which form your skull.

7

# What's inside a bone?

Compact bone

Spongy bone

Bone marrow

Periosteum

The hard white outside of a bone is called compact bone. Nerves and blood vessels of the periosteum, a thin membrane, nourish this outer layer. The layer of spongy bone inside helps keep your bones flexible. The soft marrow, found inside many bones, is like a factory producing blood cells for the whole body.

## Do you keep the same bones all your life?

Your bones are constantly rebuilding themselves—you have a new skeleton about every seven years.

# How do bones help us hear?

Tiny bones inside your ear carry sound vibrations to your brain, where they are converted into information about what you heard.

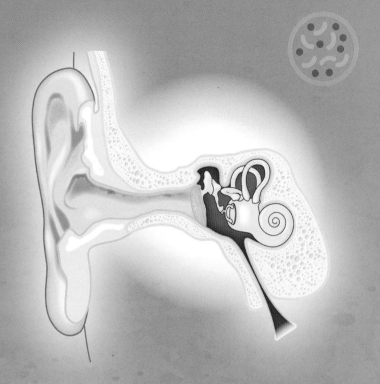

Red bone marrow

Hematopoietic stem cells (HSCs)

Red blood cells

White blood cells

Platelets

# How does bone marrow work?

Bone marrow contains red marrow and yellow marrow. Red marrow is made of stem cells that can grow into other types of cell to work where the body requires them. Millions of red blood cells are made every second by red marrow. Yellow marrow is mostly fat and as we age it replaces red marrow in bones in our arms and legs.

## Do bones scrape together?

A flexible tissue called cartilage covers bones meeting at joints. It reduces friction and lets them move more freely.

9

# Why don't bones break when you jump?

When you leap and run, your bones don't break. They're tough enough to deal with all your movements. But they aren't solid white stuff all the way through. Bones have a hard outer layer that supports your weight but is light enough to let you move. Inside, though, are living tissues performing many jobs for your whole body.

Metatarsals
(foot bones)

Heel bone

Ligament

## What joins bones together?

Bones link to other networks in the body to give it strength and support. Tough tissues called ligaments connect bones to other bones, so that you can move bits of your body. Bones are also connected to muscles, with strong bands of tissue called tendons.

### Can people make artificial bones?

Scientists have produced hard bone-like material but are still trying to find ways of linking it to blood vessels.

# Can bones bend?

Bones are flexible, so they don't snap in half at the first sign of stress. However, they don't bend very much. Instead, we move our body into different positions using the connections between bones. Your skeleton is helped by joints, muscles, tendons, and ligaments.

I'm so hip!

## Which are your body's strongest ligaments?

The ligaments connecting your hip and leg bones need to support the most weight and also need to be flexible—enough to do splits, for example.

## How do bones move?

Your bones meet each other at junctions, called joints. Some joints, like your knees, work like hinges and let bones swing back and forth. Others, like your shoulders, allow even more movement. In each case, tough tissues called ligaments attach to both bones and act like pulleys.

## What's the difference between a sprain and a strain?

Sometimes one of your joints gets twisted beyond its normal range. This movement can stretch and damage the ligaments, causing a sprain. Strains happen when you overstretch a muscle. They are very common in sports such as basketball. Both sprains and strains can often take longer to heal than a broken bone.

STRE-E-E-TCH!

13

# Do our bones grow bigger?

**Y**es! They grow bigger when you're young, making you taller and stronger. Sometimes they grow very quickly in "growth spurts." They stop getting bigger when you're in your teens. But bone-building continues all through your life. Your bones are constantly renewing themselves so that they can provide support and produce blood cells.

## How big is a growth spurt?

A typical spurt is up to 3–4 inches (8 cm) in just a few months, but some people grow up to 12 inches (30 cm) in a year.

Leg bones such as the femur are called "long bones."

# How do bones grow larger?

"Long bones" such as those in your arms and legs have growth plates at each end. Inside the plates are columns of cartilage (the same tissue as in your nose). The cartilage multiplies, turning into hard bone and pushing the plates further along. With more hardened material, the bones grow longer.

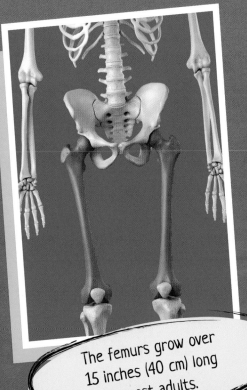

The femurs grow over 15 inches (40 cm) long in most adults.

# What makes bones stop growing?

Bone growth depends on hormones: chemicals that the body produces. You inherit growth information from your parents. This tells your body how much growth hormone to produce. When you reach puberty (becoming physically mature), a different hormone tells growth plates to fuse into hard bone, stopping any more growth.

### Do we lose bones as we grow older?

No, but some do fuse together. Babies start with more than 300 hard pieces, which are mainly cartilage. By the time you are an adult, these will have joined up to leave you with 206 bones.

# What happens if you break a bone?

Bones, like other parts of your body, are usually able to recover from serious injury. Within minutes of a break, your body starts to heal. It completes its task in stages, first stopping blood from escaping and finishing with a new length of bone where the break had been.

**Ouch!!**

### Why do you need to have a cast?

An injured bone can be knocked out of place if it is bumped, so a cast acts as a shock absorber. Sometimes, metal pins are inserted to hold a broken bone in place.

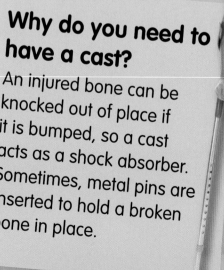

# How long does a bone take to mend?

A broken bone can take several months to heal for an adult, but a child's bone often heals within weeks. Bones contain cells that remove and replace old tissue, and other cells to build up new bone. A growing child has more "building" cells than "removing" cells, so the bone can rebuild (or heal) more quickly.

## Which is the likeliest bone to break?

The most commonly broken bone for most people is the radius bone in the wrist. Elderly people, though, often break their hips.

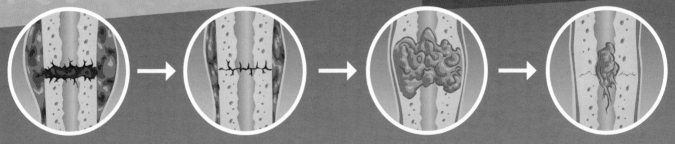

Clot forms    Connection toughens    Soft tissue builds    Fracture heals

## How does a bone heal itself?

Soon after a break, the bone forms a clot where blood vessels have become exposed. New blood vessels then join this area, turning the clot into tougher connection. Collagen (the main protein in bones) and cartilage build up, and then new cells arrive to turn these soft tissues into hard bone.

# Can bones get sick?

Any part of your body can become injured or diseased. If it happens to your bones, your body can lose mobility and support, as well as some of its ability to produce new blood cells. Some conditions arise because of wear and tear, but infections can also develop quickly.

## What diseases affect bones?

Much like other parts of the body, bones can become diseased if infections are carried in through blood vessels. Other conditions occur because people inherit them (like having weak or brittle bones) or through constant use. Arthritis often develops because the cartilage between bones becomes thinner, so that bones rub together painfully.

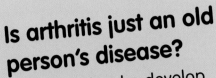

### Is arthritis just an old person's disease?

Most people who develop arthritis are in their forties or older, but young people can sometimes be affected. Proper treatment can control it.

## Do older people have weaker bones?

Bones are like factories, constantly working. They produce blood cells all the time, but as people get older some of this work slows down. Bone-building cells, which constantly renew bones, often can't keep bones as strong. Bones become less dense—and weaker—as a result.

### Do people shrink as they get older?

As people age, gravity takes its toll on the spine. The discs between the vertebrae get squeezed, so people can look a little bit shorter.

19

# How do X-rays show your bones?

Doctors can use special equipment to get clear images of your bones and other parts of your body beneath your skin. X-ray photography is the most common method of checking how your bones are developing—or healing, if they've been injured.

KER-CHINGGG!

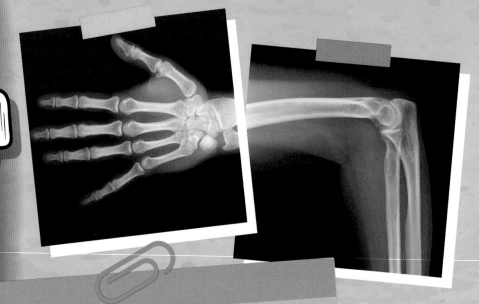

### Do X-rays just show bones?
X-ray images give clear pictures of screws and pins in joints—and sometimes even show things that people have swallowed.

## Why do bones show up so clearly?

X-rays are waves of light with more energy than the "normal" light we can see. This extra energy allows them to pass through soft tissue such as skin. Harder, denser tissue such as bones stops the waves. An X-ray machine zaps the light through the body and onto special photographic film. The bones show up as white areas where the X-rays could not reach the film.

## What else can X-rays show?

A doctor with an X-ray can see if anything is wrong inside a person, but other professionals also use this technology to save lives. If you pass your bags through an X-ray machine at an airport, the staff will be able to see the contents inside. They can check for dangerous or banned items without opening the luggage.

# Can bones be fat?

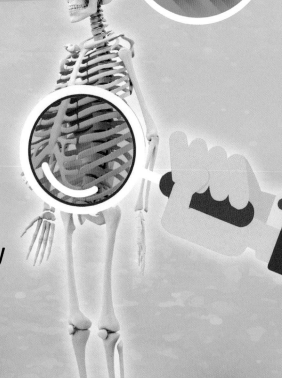

Your bones can't grow fatter, but they do store fat inside. Bones hold emergency supplies of energy, stored as fat in yellow bone marrow. They also store vital minerals that your body needs to function, and the blood cells they produce help you stay healthy and recover from injury.

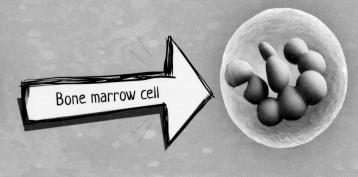

Bone marrow cell

## What is a transplant?

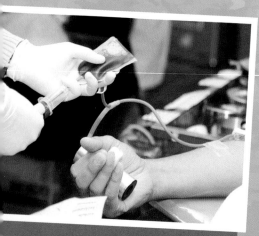

In a healthy person, bone marrow produces cells for the whole body. Some health conditions prevent this from happening properly. Healthy cells from one person's marrow can be transplanted into a sick person's body to help their marrow work better. Blood can also be taken from one person and given to another person if they need it.

## How active is bone marrow?

Red bone marrow can produce up to 5 billion blood cells each day.

## Do young bones work harder?

Nearly all of your bones contain red marrow when you're born and throughout most of your childhood. After that, the number of bones with red marrow declines. That means that adults have fewer blood-cell-producing bones than children. It's why children heal faster—and grow.

## When are bones strongest?

Young bones get stronger as part of the growing process, especially if you eat well and exercise. They are strongest in your twenties. After that, bone strength decreases unless you exercise regularly.

# How do bones stay strong?

The chemical element calcium is an important ingredient for helping your bones rebuild and stay strong. Some foods, especially dairy products (including ice cream), contain calcium. You also need vitamin D to help your body extract the calcium from food.

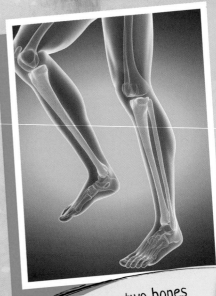

You have two bones below each knee.

24

# Why is sunshine good for bones?

Some things you eat will give you vitamin D, but sensible exposure to sunlight is the best way to get a regular dose. Chemicals in your skin can transform the sunshine into a form of vitamin D. You only need around 20 minutes, then you can move into the shade again.

## Can you eat bones?

You should avoid most bones in your food as they can damage your insides, but soft fish bones like those in canned salmon are a great source of extra calcium.

## How do helmets protect your skull?

Protective clothing and pads shield people from forces that could injure or break bones. Bike helmets help to protect your skull and your brain. Their hard outer layer spreads the force of an impact from one area. The softer, inner layer absorbs that force so that less of it reaches your head.

# Are all skeletons the same?

All but one of the 206 bones in an adult skeleton are the same in males and females. The odd one out is the pelvis, which is larger and wider in females. This is to help females with childbirth—something male bodies don't have to go through. The different shape of the pelvis helps scientists to identify skeletons as male or female.

### Does bone size matter?
Size doesn't matter, but females generally have smaller bones than males. Size is another way scientists can decide if skeletons are male or female.

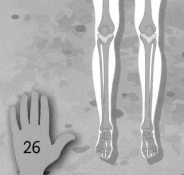

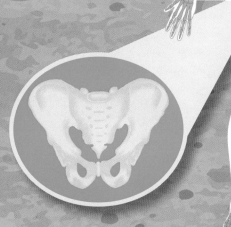

## Do animals have skeletons?

The animal kingdom is divided into two groups—vertebrates and invertebrates. All vertebrates (mammals, birds, reptiles, fish, and amphibians) have a backbone and many have a full skeleton as well, which provides a framework to support the animal's body, just like humans.

# Can we change our skeleton?

We can't grow extra bones to change our skeleton, but some people do have metal bones inside their body. This is a way of replacing natural bones that have worn out or become damaged. The most common place for a bone replacement is the hip, where the ball-and-socket joint is replaced with a metal version.

# How does everything work together?

Our bodies are made up of different systems. Each system has its own function, such as converting food into energy, or removing waste. The systems all work together to bring the human body to life.

## Circulatory system

Your heart is at the center of this system, which pumps blood around your body via veins and arteries.

## Skeletal system

All 206 bones make up the skeletal system, which supports and protects your body.

## Muscular system

Around 640 muscles in your body help you move. Your muscles are attached to your bones by tendons.

## Respiratory system

Your lungs draw in air to bring oxygen into the body and push it out to move carbon dioxide out.

## Nervous system

The brain passes messages around the body via a system of nerves. Nerves also pass messages received by your senses back to the brain.

## Excretory system

Toxins and waste materials are removed from your body by this system, which includes your kidneys and bladder.

Testes (male)

## Digestive system

This system takes in food, and breaks it down into energy and basic nutrients the body can use.

## Endocrine system

Glands in this system produce chemicals called hormones that help you grow and change your mood.

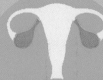

Ovaries (female)

29

# Glossary

**ancestor** An earlier type of human from which others evolved.

**arthritis** A disease that causes painful inflammation of the joints around bones.

**bone marrow** The soft tissue in the center of a bone that produces red blood cells.

**calcium** A chemical element important for helping bones stay strong.

**cartilage** Flexible tissue that acts as a shock absorber where bones meet the joints.

**cell** The smallest functioning unit in an organism. Cells join together to make tissue.

**collagen** The main protein found in bones.

**compact bone** The hard white outside of a bone.

**flat bones** Bones that are generally found in your hips, ribs and shoulder blades. They are strong to protect your vital organs.

**fossil** The remains, or an imprint of an animal or plant preserved for millions of years as stone.

**hormones** Chemicals produced by the body.

**joint** Strong connections that join bones together and allow your skeleton to move.

**ligaments** A band of strong tissue that connects the ends of bones together.

**long bones** Bones that are generally found in your fingers, toes, arms and legs; for example, the femur.

**mammals** Warm-blooded vertebrate animals with hair or fur. They give birth to live young and produce milk to nourish them.

**organ** A collection of cells that work together to perform a specific function.

**protein** One of the most important of all molecules in the body, protein is needed to strengthen and replace tissue in the body.

**short bones** Bones that are generally found in your wrists and feet to provide support and stability.

**skeleton** The framework of bones that gives the body its shape and structure.

**spine** The backbone.

**tendon** The tissue that attaches muscle to a bone.

**tissue** A collection of cells that look the same and have a similar job to do in the body.

**vertebrae** The small bones that together make up the backbone.

**X-rays** Waves of light with more energy than the normal light we can see. They can pass through soft tissue and other materials that normal light can't pass through.

# Further Information

## Further reading

**Big Book of the Body** *by Minna Lacey* (Usborne, 2016)

**Body Works** *by Anna Claybourne* (QED Publishing, 2014)

**Everything You Need to Know about the Human Body** *by Patricia MacNair* (Kingfisher, 2011)

**Guinness World Records: Amazing Body Records** *by Christa Roberts* (HarperCollins, 2016)

**How the Body Works** *by editors of DK* (Dorling Kindersley, 2016)

**Project Science: Human Body** *by Sally Hewitt* (Franklin Watts, 2012)

## Websites

PowerKids Press has developed an online list of websites related to the subject of this book. This site is updated regularly. Please use this link to access the list: **www.powerkidslinks.com/hbfaq/bones**

# Index